STUDIO PRESS BOOKS

First published in the UK in 2018 by Studio Press Books,
an imprint of Kings Road Publishing, part of Bonnier Books UK,
The Plaza, 535 King's Road, London, SW10 0SZ
www.studiopressbooks.co.uk
www.bonnierbooks.co.uk

3 5 7 9 10 8 6 4

ISBN 978-1-78741-426-6

Cartoons by Tim Whyatt

Printed in Turkey

SENIOR MOMENTS

Animal Instincts

STUDIO
PRESS

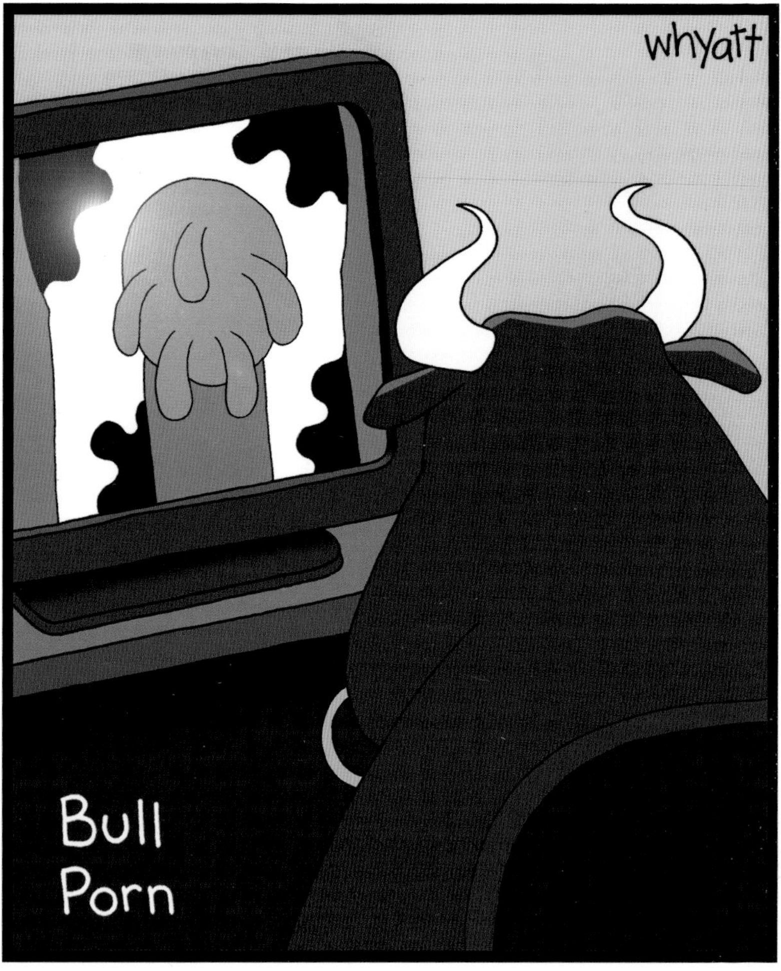
whyatt
Bull
Porn

Why dogs find humans confusing

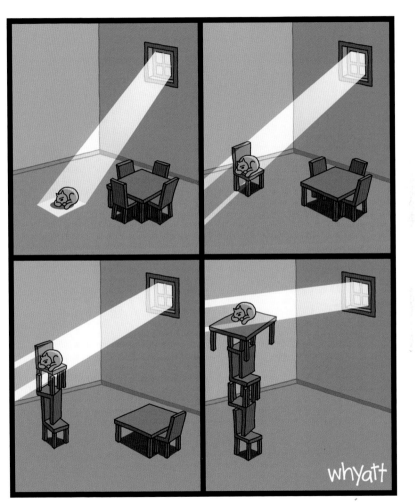

Snooze buttons for cat owners

Catholic

Catholic
Cataholic

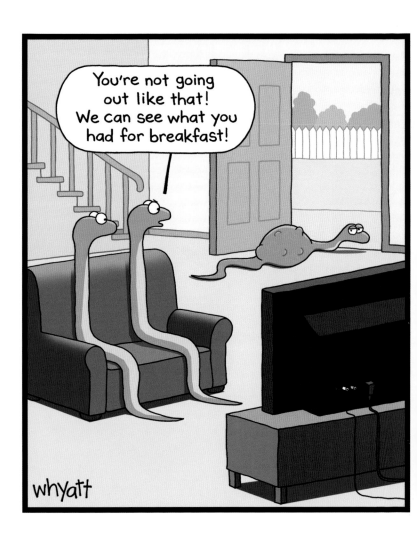

The difference between cats and dogs

Reggie was no stranger
to the international signal
for 'I'm Watching You'